RED

MW00324921

The Irrefutable Truth, Guaranteed Will Transpire in The Future.

DR. LESTER G. REID

Author, Professor, Life Coach, Entrepreneur, and Transformational Speaker.

The Author

of

"Self-promotion: A Success Winning Strategy."

&

"The Road to Personal Development and Business Venture."

Published by

Global Higher Education Institute.

RED FLAGS

The Irrefutable Truth, Guaranteed Will Transpire
in The Future.

ISBN-13: 978-1-7340601-0-2

Copyright © 2019

by

Dr. Lester Reid

All rights reserved and are never to be reproduced,
plagiarized and converted into audio or video
recording without the permission of Dr. Lester Reid.

Printed in the United States of America.

YOUR CONTRIBUTION

When you purchase this narrative directly from Dr. Lester Reid, a portion of the proceeds will be donated to a qualified charitable organization that helps at risk kids in middle and high school. Also, I am working with students who can't afford to go to college to become whatever their heart desires.

Thank you for your kind support.

Dr. Lester Reid

PREFACE

This narrative is a compilation of **RED FLAGS** that occur in our lives every single day that are guaranteed to affect us adversely or positively in the future, whether we believe it or not or whether we like or not. The **RED FLAGS** identified in this narrative will bring awareness about the things and events we may frequently overlook or take for granted, which later on may become a lifetime cost, detriment, or a blessing to our life.

This narrative addresses the **RED FLAGS** when:

- being with someone who is walking with you, but is not with you
- seeking a soulmate
- dating
- having intimacy
- being married
- dating a stripper

- dating someone who likes multiple sexual partners
- dating someone with or without kids
- being with a partner who is a habitual liar
- being with a partner who is a pretender
- being with a partner who is gay or lesbian
- being with a partner who has several sexual preferences
- investing into a relationship or marriage that's going nowhere
- your best friend deceives and betrays you
- children from previous relationship and marriage affect your future
- when family interferes with your decision to be with your soulmate and lifelong partner

The **RED FLAGS** shared in this narrative will influence us to **STOP, RECOGNIZE, ACKNOWLEDGE,** and **MAKE** some life changing decisions. This narrative will increase our awareness and compel us to pay attention and to never take our life and the life of others for granted. Recognizing and acknowledging **RED FLAGS** will certainly save us from going down a path of destruction.

My prayer and hope is that you will allow what is shared in this narrative to speak to your heart and mind and you begin to make incremental changes so that you can live a peaceful and successful life **NOW**, and don't wait until it is too late to do what will release you from making the wrong decisions that will strip you of your values, moral and principles that has been governing your life all these years. This narrative lays out the **RED FLAGS** that needs to be mitigated or eliminated from your life.

TABLE OF CONTENTS

INTRODUCTION

After reading this narrative, you will make sure that you don't take things, people and your life for granted anymore. Certainly, you will be aware of the behavior of others and how those behaviors may affect your life today and in the future. Many times, you may have sleepwalked through life and later on woken to the harsh reality and by that moment, it may have been too late to turn back the hands of time. Sometimes you had willfully blinded your eyes to the inevitable and found out later that you made a big mistake that probably will cost you the rest of your natural life. Your faith and future will always depend on your choices, and your choice will define who you are and what you are capable of doing.

You don't have the luxury or time to continually make choices that will destroy your life and the life of others. What you do today will matter in the future, whether you like it or not.

What others do to you in your life will always be before you; however, many times you choose to not acknowledge and recognize what's happening. You are not weak; you are simply telling yourself that what's happening is not important and that it will go away at some point in time, wrong! In this case, you are living a life of DENIAL which leads to the path of destruction.

To deny the inevitable is foolish and dangerous whether you are within your right mind or not. No decision is a decision and making the wrong decision may evidently determine your future. The time and resources you may have today may not be around in the future; therefore, it is important that you pay attention to the RED FLAGS that is frequently revealed and warns you of what will certainly happen in the future.

Fooling yourself every day into thinking that what you see happening before your eyes is temporary and nothing to be worried about is a mistake. If you take the time for a moment to revisit some of the events and things that had happened in your life, things that you should have taken care of earlier or prevented from ever happening in the future, you will notice, that you would have been in a better position and living a much more wholesome life today.

The question you must ask yourself is: will you continue to make the same mistakes again by not paying attention to the RED FLAGS in your life? If you are mindful and aware of the RED FLAGS in your life, think about the great accomplishments you could be enjoying each day and how much pain, sorrow, and discomfort you would save yourself from going through for the rest of your life. Your happiness and well-being are worth more than you can ever imagine. You have to make it clear to yourself that RED FLAGS are the indicators of who a person is and the same events and behaviors will reoccur in the future. Remember, you can't change a person, however, you can make a change in your own life and make it beautiful worthwhile.

Whether you look for **RED FLAGS** or not, they will always be there staring you right in the face, waiting for you to recognize them. You must make decisions based on the knowledge and information you have experienced throughout your life. **RED FLAGS** do not draw attention to themselves; however, **RED FLAGS** are there to tell us, pause and examine what's going on in order to make the right move and decision. Then we must make a decision that will either be a benefit or a curse to us in the future. No matter how much you love someone or care about them passionately or would love to be with that person in the future, it is important that you recognize that their actions will ultimately bring a blessing or a curse to your life whether you like it or not, and at that point, it may be too late for you to decide to opt out.

A person may look beautiful and have everything that you need or want, but that person may not be the best person to spend the rest of your life with, no matter how caught up you are with your emotions. Many have lost their lives, sacrificed their future, or are paying the price to this day, yet they still allow themselves to be connected with the person who is bringing them down a path of destruction. There are some things in life that will never change, and above all, some things you may not be able to retrieve once it's gone. Therefore, it is important that you value your life and the decisions you make for the purpose of living a wholesome and prosperous life in the future.

CHAPTER ONE

RED FLAGS - Soulmate/Life Long Partner

What are Red Flags?

The irrefutable evidence is revealed and is guaranteed to manifest in the future.

Who are Soulmates?

These are two people whose souls, spirits, bodies and minds are intimately tied together which exhibit the abilities to telepathically, telekinetically and spiritually connect with each other from anywhere in the world without even being in each other's presence. The soulmates are so connected and intertwined, they can feel each other's love and pain from a distance.

Who is a Lifelong Long Partner?

These are two people who have a lifelong history of bonding of their soul, spirit, body, and mind and having each other's best interests at heart. They maintain an unbroken intimate agreement which requires them to work together for a common and greater good. They live purposefully with and for each other, no matter how challenging life may be at that point in time.

Choosing a soulmate or lifelong intimate partner is the most important choice that a person could ever make, since they are connecting themselves with someone for the rest of their natural life. Having a soulmate or lifelong partner is so critical, that if you overlook understanding the requirements and the significance of who a soulmate or partner is, then certainly it will be a tremendous cost to you in the future. Nowadays, people have overlooked the fact that the choice they make will determine whether their life will be filled with joy, peace and success or with pain, sorrow, disappointment and destruction. Your life is the most important thing in the world no matter what others may say or think about you. Whoever you connect your soul or your entire being with, will help to either build or destroy you and what you stand for that is important to you. It is your business to make sure that you are in control of your soul, spirit, body and mind and recognize that the choices you make will not only bring happiness or sorrow to your life, but also to the life of the person you are sharing your life with.

A soulmate is divinely connected to a person who is connected to their soul and heart and such experience is telekinetic, telepathic and sometimes unexplainable. No matter where both persons are they both think, feel and sense each other from a distance. Such experience between two people is inevitable, powerful and should never to be taken for granted. A soulmate can tell, see, and discern their partner's needs, interests and everything about that person from a distance and cater to those needs selflessly because their soulmate is divinely connected to him or her. When searching for a soulmate or a lifelong intimate partner, it is important that you be very patient, considerate, confident, and have faith, no matter what. God will send you the person that you rightfully deserve, and you don't need to be with every and any person who does not connect with your soul, body and mind. Sometimes, it may take months and years for you to find the person who will be your soulmate. In many cases you don't have to be seeking someone to be your soulmate, but such person will show up in your life at some point unexpectedly. Your soul will make a connection with your soulamte and you will know for sure that the person is for you.

PARTNERSHIP

When you get involved with someone, it is important that you understand that you should get yourself involved with someone who will be your lifelong partner. A lifelong partner is someone who understands your needs and you understand their needs. There is a bond and a spiritual connection between both of them to support and facilitate each aspiration and dreams. Both partners should always acknowledge, recognize and endeavor to support and please each other wholeheartedly. They should strive to build up each other and be there for each other through the good and bad times. In a relationship or in marriage both persons must acknowledge and appreciate each other as partners.

When you connect yourself with someone who is presumed to be your soulmate, that person also should be seen, recognized, and acknowledge as your lifelong intimate partner of which both people are in agreements with each other to see that each person become successful by supporting each other's dreams, aspirations, and anything that seems like it would be a benefit to each other.

When there's a partnership between both parties in a relationship or in marriage, anything is possible for them to accomplish together in the future. Partnership between both parties is a work in progress. There is a continual need for much effort, dedication, focus, sacrifice, dreams, aspirations, and passion in order for that long-life intimate partnership to grow and blossom into something that is joyful and meaningful.

IN YOUR BEST INTEREST

When soulmates decide and consider their partner's decision and contribution, it's a remarkable thing to do which bring togetherness and happiness in the long run. Being selfless and considerate are characteristics that develops thecrelationship into something outstanding and powerful beyond both partners' ability to conceive or imagine. When each partner or soulmate recognizes that their partner or soulmate is acting in their best interest, then their soulmate will do almost anything for him or her. No matter what the cost may be or no matter what it will take, a soulmate will do what's necessary to please and satisfy his or her soulmate from the core and the depths of their soul. Such characteristics are lost in our society today and many of us are living in fear and doubt regarding connecting our life with another person or even to get married in a time such as this.

Working on operating in the best interest of your soulmate is the most important thing you could ever do. That will create hope, confidence and optimism within a relationship or a marriage that is destined for success and prosperity. When you are connecting your soul to another person who is in your best interest, it's like arriving at a place you have always want to go. The dream of finally getting to where you want to be and enjoying the moment and not trading it in for anything else in life, is worth the journey. Being selfless, considerate, and thoughtful are three characteristics that soulmates possess in order for there to be a bright future to look forward to.

FAITHFULNESS AND LOYALTY

In our society today, more and more people are looking for faithfulness in the person they're with romantically. Without faithfulness there is no hope in the future for both people to enjoy the fruits of their labor. You may have witnessed a couple being madly in love with each and one day those moments end because of unfaithfulness and disloyalty. Faithfulness and loyalty is the substratum of a successful and healthy relationship which must bring happiness and joy to both partners.

Cheating, deceiving, withholding information, and withholding truth and facts from a partner or soulmate is not only wrong, but it also takes both people down a path of destruction. What's the use devoting so much time, energy and the resources into a partnership, then all of a sudden, such beautiful thing and experiences comes to an end? That's meaningless. It is important that the couple seek professional counseling that will help to overcome those difficult moments that have affected relationship negatively and focus on improving the things that derailed the partnership. Both soulmates should focus on working together for a common goal and support each other's best interests. All good things will happen when both people have trust, confidence and hope in each.

It is important to understand that when your soulmate loses faith and confidence in you because of disloyalty and infidelity, it is very difficult for them to trust you wholeheartedly and maintain their confidence in you. So, no matter how much of a risk a person may take without thinking before doing something that is wrong, it is important that in the sub-consciousness of our minds we realize that once that confidence trust and faith is violated, it can be sometime impossible to restore. It is important then, that before someone does anything or say anything that's going to violate the relationship, he or she must think about the consequences of their action and how much it will cost the relationship after investing so much time, money, confidence and trust.

Never take for granted your soulmate, your partner, and your future. After all it's not always about you. It's always about both of you that really matters. Whenever you're in a relationship, it is important that you recognize that no matter what you do to one another, your partner will reciprocate the same to you. One has to think that they cannot do or say anything without considering the contribution of their soulmate or partner. Dating and maintaining a relationship should be considered a training ground for the real thing which is engagement then marriage. When you start practicing being open and honest to each other about the past and the present, this will enable both parties to recognize that they trust each other and have each other's best interest at heart.

Faithfulness, trust, and loyalty are the foundation of a successful relationship and marriage. Without these great qualities, nothing will work, nothing will last and nothing will bring joy and happiness to each other's heart.

FAMILY AND FUTURE

After many weeks of dating and spending quality time getting to know each other, it is important that both persons begin to discuss whether or not they want to start building a family. Will the relationship lead to a future that is worth the time and the investment? At some point the dating process will come to an end and a new beginning starts with both people making that next step to become married with a mind to start building a family together. In a time, such as this many people are scared to think about getting married after dating and some are even more scared of talking about getting ready to start a family before getting married. However, because of the values and the principles that one group believes, it is imperative that like-minded people think about a wholesome and prosperous future together in the future. When you really think about it, having a partner, a soulmate, is a beautiful thing and taking the time to get to know each other causes the love to grow and blossom into something beautiful. Each person becomes appreciative of the other. Then it's important that both people make the next move to become one in holy matrimony. The future will bring all kinds of challenges and of course it will also bring a lot of blessings and opportunities that will make it worth the investing of time, energy, and resources together.

After getting married, after becoming one, after realizing that both people have all things in common, and also recognize that both individuals can be a blessing and a benefit instead of a burden or liability to each other, then both individual will agree that they have made the best move ever to let their world become one and everything else revolves around them and how they start that new life together. The opportunities that await both individuals are an endless field of of rewards and opportunities. So therefore, after you have recognized and understand your soulmate and your partner and have made that extra move to be with in the future, it is important that both individuals agree at some point in time during the dating process to finally make that step to be one and also to make all possibilities become their adventure. The future will always be bright regardless of all the stumbling blocks that may come your way. However, when both people are in it together and overcome those obstacles together, they can celebrate their victory over those stumbling blocks. Never doubt yourself that building a future with someone you love and you care for is worth every effort and every sacrifice you could ever make in your entire life, for the greater good of yourself, your soulmate or partner, and for anyone else that's a part of your life. Dating at some point must come to an end and the new beginning of being engaged and becoming husband-and-wife should be the next great move for a wholesome and prosperous life together.

GOALS, ACHIEVEMENTS AND CELEBRATION

When soulmates recognize that they have to work together as partners toward their shared goals: being faithful, reliable, loyal and honest, then both people should set goals and achieve them together, and then later on celebrate their success with each other together. Relationships requires a lot of work, effort, love, and an investment of time and resources. In order for a relationship or a marriage to grow and to blossom into something beautiful, both partners have to set goals, privatize their goals, and work on their goals together. They must recognize that one day they both will celebrate each other success due to the fact that they have put their heart, soul, mind, resources and body into achieving things together. That's worth exploring. After working together as a partner, as a soulmate and achieving things together, it is imperative that both people really look out for the ultimate results that are going to help them to grow and develop and maximize their skills and abilities, talents, and credentials together for the greater good of both of them and those who also is a part of their lives and their success.

If a couple fails to work together, fails to set goals, fails to achieve things together over the years, then look out for all kinds of elements to come in and destroy what they began and worked together so hard to achieve initially. When there's no goals, no drive, no passion, no inspiration, no togetherness, certainly something or someone will come in and destroy or derail the success of what both people should accomplish together for the greater good of themselves and those who are a part of their lives. Goals, achievements, success and celebration should be the main priority between soulmates and they should endeavor to protect those characteristics or attributes with all their heart and soul and mind and their body and spirit and to make sure nothing and no one prevents them from achieving the things that they should achieve together and celebrate with each other in the future.

LIMITING FRIENDS

Whenever you're dating someone and their friends maybe from elementary school, middle school, or high school tends to take precedence in their life then it is important that yourself and your partner begin to discuss matters. Especially when it has to do with limiting the influences of friends during the dating process. It's not easy telling your partner, your soulmate to reduce the level of influence they may have on your partner, your soulmate, and moreover overlooking the long history of their relationship prior to your relationship with your soulmate. However, discussions are to be had, understanding has to be established, and agreements need to be made. You and your partner or soulmate should understand that you are getting ready to start the future and the emphasis should be on both of you to spend quality time to get to know each other get to build each other and get to do a lot of things together for the mere fact of getting to appreciate and love each other wholeheartedly. Both you and your partner should come to an agreement that there's going to be limitation as to how much your friends influence your lives and how much time is given to friends during the dating process.

Nothing is wrong with your partner spending time with friends. I' mean taking the time to enjoy moments away from yourself. The same should be for your partner to allow you to have time and moments with your friends to do things, to go places, and to enjoy at least the remaining moments together with them, knowing that in the future you are going to spend the rest of your time with your soulmate and partner together as one. If your friends are being dismissive of your soulmate and partner's contribution and involvement in your life, then it has to be known to them that you want them to accept and respect your relationship, your partnership, and possibly your marriage; therefore, they need to let that union grow and blossom into something great. Limiting friend's engagement, contribution, and influence is very important. If that does not take place, then certainly that will have a negative impact on the growth of the relationship and a marriage and possibly can destroy the great thing that you both have been building together for a long time.

When a relationship is arriving to a point where it's now time to get married, it is now important that friends of both parties begin to support each other in every aspect and to wish both of you Godspeed and blessing upon your future and recognize that all that is getting ready to happen is good. Remember: you are in charge of your relationship with your friends and therefore you have the power to let your friends know your position, and your plans for the future with your soulmate and partner, and it is imperative that they develop their appreciation and support for the new venture you're going to explore with your soulmate in the future. in most cases, your friends and your soulmate friends will respect and appreciate your position even so when you are especially the leader in your friendship with your friends.

LIMITING FAMILY

It is very difficult to limit your family involvement in your relationship with your partner, especially seeing that your family has always been there for you or your family may have been there for you most of the time during your personal development. Some of us may not have had parents or guardians involved in our lives, however we may have had someone who may have influenced our lives in some shape or form. As a result, we consider that person or persons to be family. Now that you're going through the dating process then you have reached a point in your life where you have to draw the line. Your mother and father or other family members may tell you what to do and what not to do, I can give some positive advice that will help you to make good decisions; however, at the end of the day, it's up to you to make your own decisions, and live with those choices you make thereafter. That is why it's important that when you're choosing a soulmate or lifetime partner, you take the time to get to know that person and to check out your partner just to make sure that you understand their past, their present, and possibly have an idea of what their future may look like.

After you have come to an understanding of who your partner and soulmate is. and you have recognized that that's the person you going to spend the rest of your life with, it is important that you let your family understand that you are the one who is going to make all your decisions and you're asking them to respect your position and your decisions regardless of how they feel and think about you and that person you are going to spend the rest of your life with in the future. Family will always try to be there for you or try to destroy what you have worked so hard to put together because their jealousy or their personal dislike towards. Regardless, it is important that you know who you're with and who you going to spend the rest of your life with, and make sure that after you figure out who you're going to be with, you will let it be known with much confidence that you have finally made up your mind and you want to go forward with your decision to be one with that person for the rest of your natural life.

Your family has to take the backseat and allow you to do what you desire to do, and they have to respect your decision and your choices. They must be supportive of your plans whether they like it or not. Remember, you are the leader in the relationship you have with your family, regardless of the age and seniority your parents may have. It is important that you take the lead in in your family relationship. At the end of the day, you are the sole decision maker for the path you're getting ready to take with your soulmate and partner in the future. Standing up for yourself and your soulmate regardless of anyone's perception and feeling towards you is important and both of you should always make it your business to be there for each other and support each other no matter what others may say, think or do to prevent you from venturing into a bright future together.

SEPARATING FROM EX-MATES

When you're getting ready to start a new relationship with someone, it is important that your previous relationship with other ex-mate (s) come to an end, due to the fact that you have respect for the new person you want to spend the rest of your life with in the future. Your life cannot be shared with multiple parties at the same time, and your interest should be directed towards one person, and that person only you want to spend the rest of your life with. Before you begin something new, you must put away the past experiences and focus on the future especially with your new partner. Otherwise, you will make a mess of the future and when it gets to that point there is a possibility there would not be a bright future between you and your expected partner and soulmate in the future.

Sometimes we move from one relationship to another without thinking about what went wrong in the previous or never tried to figure out what needed to be fixed before getting into a new relationship with someone else.

It is important that ex-mate relationships no longer play a role in your life as you try to build a new future with your new soulmate and partner who is going to be your life partner for the rest of your natural life. Your new life partner is expected to do the very same, denying and forsaking all others and making it his or her business to build a wholesome and fruitful life together with you with the expectation of reaping blessings and benefits together in the future. All respect and confidence are due to the relationship you're building and getting ready to expand, with no compromise, action, or interruption by the past or anything that may involve the present or in the future that will hinder the growth and development of your relationship and marriage with the person you intend to spend the rest of your life with in the future.

STRENGHTS AND WEAKNESSES

It is important that when you're dating someone you take the time to observe and understand their strengths and weaknesses. After all this is important for you to do, so knowing that the person you are spending time with will eventually one day be a lifetime partner and soulmate. It is important that you identify and recognize your partner's strengths and praised him or her almost immediately and often when you recognize it. This enables them to see that you are appreciating them for who they are and for their strengths and also how much they can become valuable to you. Your partner's strengths may be the exact thing you need in your life. After all you may lack those strengths yourself and you may really need those strengths to help you to be a better person. For example, you may not be a good money manager. Spending may be your weakness and you may have been struggling greatly in this area or a very long time. Instead of saving and investing, you spend frequently and even waste money at times. You definitely need someone stronger in your life to help you improve in this area.

You may frequently find yourself overextended which ultimately will bring ruin to your life and possibly any other person's life. You may also not be good at maintaining a clean and safe home possibly because you were not taught how to do so when you were younger. Examples like these may pose a problem to any person you may connect yourself with, and also may be a problem for you because those areas in your life really need to be cool in order for you to live a wholesome and beautiful life in the future. Meeting someone with those qualities and characteristics may ultimately help you to improve in those areas as well as help you bring out the best that has been hidden inside of you for very long time. Sometimes when you're single you may tend to not hear about the things that really matters in life that needs to be addressed and taken care of; however, you may live a carefree life that doesn't require many changes and improvements, whether you noticed it or not. Your partner may have an influence in your life and help you evolve into someone great, however living single, you failed to make it your business to explore those strengths that are critical to human development and growth.

The weakness in your partner's life and your life maybe each other's strengths and can be a great source of support and bring out the best in each other regardless of the weaknesses that are there. Weaknesses do not necessarily mean that the relationship has ended. Rather, the weaknesses are indicators that tells you or your partner that those fears can be improved once you make it your business to work together to improve those weaknesses and bring out the best in each other. Your partner and yourself should agree that when they see the strengths and weaknesses in each other, it is your business to make sure that both of you are there for each other for the greater good of the relationship or marriage that will blossom into something greater than yourselves.

It is important that has you think about connecting your life with someone that you love and care about, you begin to recognize that your partner will not be temporary in your life, but that they'll be a part of your life as a lifelong partner and soulmate forever. After becoming one and working together, supporting each other, and growing together, you both have to agree make a good agreement to work in each other's best interests and continually share your success with each other. There is no room for mistakes when choosing a soulmate. After all your life, your family, your resources, and your future will all be at stake. Who you invite into your life and share your body mind and soul with should not only be temporary but should be a part of your entire human development and achievements in the future.

CHAPTER TWO

RED FLAGS – Dating

During the dating process, it's important that one understand that having all things in common is very important. You may think that all things or most things in common is not that important - not until you get yourself so involved with the person. Then you realize that there's so many differences between both of you. By then it may be too late to back out. Perhaps you should back out of the relationship, think things through very carefully. After all, it is your business to make sure that whoever you're going to put your time and energy and resources into, is worth every effort, every dollar, and everything that you could put your heart into. Remember, who you choose today and the time, energy, resources, and anything else you put into that dating process will either be a benefit or a cost to you in the future. It is important that you realize that you don't have all the time in the world to make bad choices and then look forward to doing the right thing or the best thing in the future. You can start by thinking about what's important to you when you meet someone and then desire to spend your time and resources with that person, with the intention of knowing that what you're doing today and the days ahead will contribute to what you're looking for in the future. Having all things in common or most things in common is imperative and is not up for a compromise or a debate.

For example, you and that person might have similar interests in music, traveling, careers, or you might both enjoy going out together and have similar career or college ambitions. Simple things like these are never to be taken for granted nor overlooked, simply because they mean so much to you and that person. Once the person you're dating possesses the same interests, characteristics, goals, ambitions, ideologies, and faith, then it's quite simple that you will put more into the dating process by doing things that makes both of you feel comfortable and happy with each other. After all it's all about what satisfies and pleases each other simultaneously, without any controversy or disagreements. Asking questions and observing the person you are dated carefully over a period of time will help you to decide whether or not it's going to be a short-term or long-term dating process of which you take very seriously, after all, your future and your life depend on the choices you make during the dating process.

It makes no sense to fool yourself to think that because the person makes you feel good or you are attracted to them or they give you things or they satisfy your emotions at that moment will change the fact that all that should matter to you most should never be replaced by a temporary fix and convenience at any given time. It is important that you already have a mindset of what you're looking for. This is what I call having a strategic plan for your future by paying attention to the red flags that are there and then take swift action with no delay. Recognize, acknowledge and make good choices that will ultimately bring a benefit to you in the future. You have to value yourself and value your decisions since your future depends on how well you handle yourself during dating.

BACKGROUND CHECK

Does knowing something about the person you are dating means anything to you? The person you meet and date today has a long history that you need to know in order for you to dedicate the rest of your life with that person in the future. You have to ask questions. You have to search for information about that person, and then later on you have to decide, after gathering information about the person's background as to whether not you're going to commit yourself to such a person. When you develop an understanding about a person based on their historical background and personal observation, you can then decide within yourself whether or not you're making the best choice pertaining to your life. A person's emotional, psychological and spiritual background should certainly be understood in order for you to decide whether or not you're going to connect your soul, spirit and being with the person you are dating. You have to find out if the person is financially responsible or not. You have to find out if the person is willing to work to make an honest living. You have to certainly find out whether or not they're capable of sustaining wholesome and pure relationship and possibly marriage in the future.

Checking a person's credit worthiness, their relationship with their parents or family, what may have transpired during their previous relationship, find out if this person is faithful and trustworthy or not, or can you trust and rely on this person or not are very important things you must find out and know in order for you to determine what your future may turn out to be. A background check is a must and should never be ignored. There are those who will withhold critical information from you that will impair your decision making. It is imperative that that you make it your business to ask questions, to inquire and search and to observe in order for you to gather critical information about the person you are dating today, so that you can make the best choice for your own life. Remember the background check helps you to become aware, develop understanding, and to make a decision that is going to propel your life into a positive or negative direction.

You might not see the relevance of doing a background check right now, maybe because you're so in love and might be happy with what's going on now. However, the day will come when you realize that the person does not believe in working to make a livelihood, saving or investing for the future, or you find out that the person has dark secrets that may affect your life negatively. By then you'll be so traumatized and some may want to kill yourself after finding out the truth later on during dating process or during marriage. There are those individuals who believed that if you didn't ask then they shouldn't tell you. You may experience during the dating process and or marriage that the person purposely has been keeping you in the dark and rob you of your choice in the matter. Don't be foolish! Take matters into your own hand to find out more about the person you are dating and possibly getting married to in the future.

UNEQUAL YOKE

Have you ever been in a situation where you're dating somebody and you find out that there's so many things that work against the relationship than works for the relationship? Or have you seen or known someone who have dated someone, and they constantly argue or fight with each other, or they can never agree with each other about a lot of things? Have you witnessed a relationship or marriage where both people are so unhappy with each other to the point they don't even touch each other romantically or intimately? Well, those are red flags to look for in a relationship. Being unequally yoked means that both individuals have different values or one may not have values, or both. Perhaps you do not have a value system that is pure and will bring benefits success and greatness towards their lives.

Being unequally yoked will never keep both individual together to the end of time. Many people get into relationships because they like each other, or they are sexually attracted to each other, or they may have been in a vulnerable situation. Therefore, they allow their emotions to get the best of them. A temporary fix is never the best solution to any problems during the dating process. The most effective way to find out if both of you are equally are unequally yoked, is to make a list together of the things that you both have in common and the things you don't have in common. From there on you can decide on whether or not you want to be with the person in the future. I am certain, that many of us have witnessed people become victims in their relationship before even getting married.

Could things be prevented from happening by first taking the time to pay attention to the red flags before joining the dating process and to make sure that the choice that has been made will be a benefit and a cost to that person's life ultimately? If you think that going against the inevitable, which is in this case being equally yoked, will make things better, think again. Remember what you do today during the dating and relationship process will determine the outcome in the future. So, it is imperative that you pay attention to the red flags during the dating process and to pay attention to the things that are more important to you and to try to observe and recognize the difference between both for you and make a good decision thereafter. It is not worth you enjoying the ride or the moment during the dating process or relationship and keep on ignoring the fact that you're going to run into a lot of challenges that eventually will destroy the relationship in the future. You have to pay attention to what's going on now and take notes in order for you to make a better choice that's going to work in your favor in the long run.

COMPROMISING

Compromising what you believe and what you stand for will not only make you uncomfortable but also make you feel like you have made the worst choice in your life. When you know what is to be done, what is right, and what is best and works out for the greater good for everybody, then you toss that aside completely because you're trying to keep the peace between you and the person you're dating or in a relationship with. Pretty soon you will begin to have doubts and question yourself about the choice you have made. When you start to compromise your integrity, confidence, faith, beliefs, principles, and standards, then all that you have worked so hard for to give in to someone who does not share similar characteristics, ambitions and value as you do, then ultimately later on one day you'll come to your senses and make the right choice. However, it may come with a cost: pain and emotional breakdown. Yes, some things you will compromise because you yourself may need improvement in those areas. Still, you have to decide within yourself that what is going to work out for the best for everyone regardless of your personal gain. You have to compromise or learn from what has been shared by your partner so that everyone can grow and blossom into something beautiful.

Selling out your belief, your soul, and your future is not worth you doing since your life is the most important thing. When you're with the person who you're dating or in a relationship with, it is important that in order for you to develop and grow to become better than what you think you are, you must learn from your partner and appreciate the values that he or she has to share with you for the greater good of the relationship during that time. Compromising for the greater good of everybody is better than not compromising for the sake of selfishness. When you realize that your partner is not being considerate of your contribution to the relationship and totally ignores the values or the standards you stand for, then it may be time for you to vacate regardless of your emotional or financial attachment to that person. Remember, your future is on the line here, and you have what it takes to decide on how your future is going to turn out with or without the person you are dating or in a relationship with. Yes, it may be hard to give up on the relationship and your love for someone you deeply want to be with in the future and someone who really me makes you feel happy and comfortable.

You must understand that no matter what, the beginning is important, the process is relevant, but, the ending is way more significant than how you started out. Do not sell out the things that are more important to you in life just for a temporary fix that later on will be dissolved and once again you find yourself at the beginning, starting over maybe with someone else new in your life. Start paying attention to the red flags while you're dating the person of interest.

ATTRACTION AND REPULSION

Almost every person who is thinking about getting into a relationship and possibly marriage is attracted to another person based on their physical appearance, how the make them feel, their financial security, and for cultural or religious purposes. Whatever the reasons are for you to be attracted to another person, it is important to know that the eyes and ears can be misled, and one may end up paying the price later on in the future. It is important that you choose someone that you are attracted to for the right reasons instead of having someone in your life that you are not attracted to you, regardless of the fact that they may bring great some value to your life in some shape or form.

At some point in your life you may have been attracted to someone that you're deeply in love, or been with someone who made you feel so good about them or someone you may have known who have been through those experiences and later on realized that they had made a poor choice just by going after what they were attracted to at that time. Nevertheless, it is important that whoever you are attracted to should bring some type of value to your life, and that you're happy with who they are instead of fooling yourself into thinking that there is going to be a bright future between the both of you. You have to be true to yourself and be honest to the person you are dating. Most women already have it within their mind that they need to be with a guy that has some type of physical feature or appearances that will appeal and complement them, maybe because of their infatuation or insecurity or just pure liking of someone that really appeals to their emotion, feelings, and persona.

Let's face it, there are a lot of people who enjoy being with someone they are dating, based on the benefits that he can earn from the person versus being attracted to them physically and emotionally. If you really think about it, it's like taking that person for granted and setting our lives back many years, instead of living a wholesome life now that leads into the future. Time is very important. Once it's gone it never can be repeated or regained. Therefore, it is important that we understand that time is very important with what we do with it today, as well as with the resources we have or may invest into a relationship. It is important that you be true to yourself and the person you're with by letting them know whether or not you are physically, emotionally, spiritually, financially attracted to them. We all learned that honesty is the best policy. Whether you believe that truism or not, being honest, truthful, and sincere may cause the person you are dating to appreciate and respect what you are sharing with them for the benefit of each other's future.

If you ask the person you are dating to be honest with you about being attracted to you, then the expectation is that they tell you the truth and you be ready to handle the truth. If you notice that the person is not spending time with you and is cheating on you, then you may have to look into whether or not they are attracted to you and really want to spend the rest of their life with you. You have to stop, recognize, acknowledge and decide about what's more important: ignoring what is happening or fooling yourself into thinking that it will get better during the dating process. Bear in mind: the person you are dating maybe turned off by something you did or did not do that is of great importance to them. It may be in your best interest to ask questions and get to the bottom of things before things get out of control. Communication is critical and must be valued between you and the person you are dating.

LOVE AND INFATUATION

Sometimes we can be consumed with being in love and told to ignore the red flags that are occurring during the dating process. Sometimes you may find yourself in a situation where instead of actually loving the person you may be infatuated with them or obsessed with the person and find it very difficult to see your life without the person in it. Many people who are in the situation of infatuation or obsession find him or herself in a position where they make life more difficult for the person they are dating and even for themselves. Sometimes you may find yourself in a situation where you're so caught up in the person and that you totally ignore the fact that so many things are going on that are not healthy for yourself or for that person.

The person also could be madly in love with you but on the other hand you find yourself reciprocated and decide within yourself that you're not going to remove yourself from being obsessed with the person or the person being obsessed which later on can become a problem. "Stubborn Love" is a beautiful thing, but it can become a problem when you are in love with someone who is not good for you. You may be in love with someone who has a terrible past, a terrible temper, a criminal background, or someone who will be a detriment to you. For some strange reason, you may call that love, but it actually be you're just infatuated with the person based on how they make you feel and what they have done for you.

If you're in a relationship someone who is abusing you verbally or physically, you should do your best to get out of the relationship before it gets worse. Those two items are clear red flags that should tell you that the future will not be bright with you and that person when you're dating or in a relationship. If that person can be verbally or physically abusing you now, can you imagine if you guys become one or living together or finalizing your union? How much more will that person do to you in the future? Love is never blind, nor is love confused. Love make you love someone about your art and that person in response to the same towards you. Love is not a one-way street. It requires reciprocation and maintenance just to make sure that love does not gets destroyed in the future. Never confuse love and infatuation; otherwise, you'll have a rude awakening and an experience that may cost you the rest of your life. Love is pure and innocent, but it is your business to make sure that it's never taken for granted or destroyed by the by another person who does not share the same feelings and emotions as you do as it pertains to love.

If the person you are dating or in a relationship loves you and care about you, then they should maintain doing so. We love them with our heart and soul though no one is perfect. It is your business to safeguard the love between you and the person and to make sure nothing and no one comes between the both of you or destroy what you have put together over a period of time. If you realize that your love is taken for granted and not appreciated then that that is a red flag that you should not overlook and ignored. Such a red flag happening now during the relationship should be acknowledged, and a decision needs to be made with no delay and no doubt. Remember: what you do today will determine what your future will be. Whether you believe it or not, the red flags will reveal itself again in the future.

DATING WITH KIDS

Dating someone with children and later on deciding to be one with that person in a relationship or getting married will certainly change your future forever. It is important that you understand that in relationship or marriage the role of each person needs to be clearly identified and respected from the very beginning. The man obviously should maintain the role of a leader in the relationship and set an example to the kids as well as the mother be an example to the children and maintain that support system that will enable the family to be successful in the future. Bringing children into a new relationship and or marriage needs to be well thought out and explored and a decision is to be only made by both parties. To maintain the relationship, they must agree that respect, leadership, support and trust is critical in the relationship or marriage. Both parties must realize that they're bringing two families together, and it is important that both persons and the relationship understand each other and understand the children that are going to be a part of the equation, and they have to decide over a period of time before even thinking about getting married or whether or not they can be together after learning the strengths and weaknesses of the children as well as of each partner in the relationship.

Both partners in the relationship must come to terms with the reality that the man has to assume leadership over all children - not just his own but all children - and the mother should be able to operate as a mother and possibly a wife in order for both to function as a couple that is raising two families to become one. Now, if you are dating with kids and you noticed that your partner's children have no respect for you, and you find yourself in a situation where you cannot maintain your role in the relationship while dating and also you realize that your partner is not allowing you to play your part that is rightly required of any relationship or marriage that involve kids, then it is imperative that you recognize that if that is going on now, it will certainly continue in the future. If either parent in the relationship does not allow each partner to preside, lead, teach, instruct, encourage or motivate the child, then that's a clear indication that you will not be able in the future to operate in the manner that is required of you as an adult and partner. Patience, understanding, respect, loyalty, faithfulness, leadership and support is required of both parties in the relationship to guide, provide, and protect the children so that they can grow up in a functional environment that is going to bring a blessing to the children's life in the future.

If the children in the relationship have no respect and appreciation for you in their lives, and your partner does nothing to improve the situation, then such a **RED FLAG** is telling you that you will for certain experience such behaviors continually within the relationship. **RED FLAGS** are never to be overlooked and taken for granted; after all, they will occur again in the future. Do what is necessary so that you don't end up living a miserable life in a relationship that will work against you versus working for you and your well-being. Why should anyone commit to relationship and a partner with kids from a prior relationship or marriage and experience all kinds of obstacles that are **RED FLAGS**, unhappiness and pain? Don't fool yourself, such indicators will continue throughout the relationship or marriage all the way to the end. Paying attention to the **RED FLAGS** and actually do something about it for your own peace of mind and sake is work every effort and resolution. Do what you must do by deciding and enjoy the outcome even if it hurts for a moment

CHAPTER THREE

RED FLAGS – Marriage

When getting married it's important that we understand that the person we are getting married to is going to be your lifelong partner, and it's important that we choose our partner very carefully. Otherwise, you may end up paying the price later. Should you notice that the person you're getting married to is unfaithful, untrustworthy, or unreliable, you should think it through before you proceed with the marriage. At the same time, if the person may give you even more indicators of doubt, you should put the wedding on hold. Going through the dating process and getting engaged afterwards requires immediate focus and your immediate attention, before you make the ultimate step to be married to a person who you going to share the rest of your life with. Marriage is an honorable thing, and it is expected that both people bring value, understanding, love, partnership, honesty, and faithfulness into the marriage regardless of the fact that things may happen after getting married that may cause you to reconsider marriage. Marriage requires each person to respect and appreciate and love each other regardless of how each other's weaknesses may reveal themselves, it is important that both people recognize and value the strengths more than highlighting the weaknesses and make those weaknesses a stumbling block that may end up causing the marriage to fall apart in the first place.

Now that you are married it is important that each partner in the relationship work together for common goal and a common good with the intention of overcoming together all roadblocks and obstacles that will work itself against the marriage. Knowing that there are forces that will work against the marriage, it is important that both partners watch over each other's life by ensuring that these forces and obstacles does not affect their partner or each other. There are issues that are going to involve you in the marriage that will cause both partners to evolve and in many cases those issues end up taking precedence over the marriage and ultimately destroys the marriage. Marriage is like a ship. It goes in one direction at a time, and there's someone expected to steer the ship to its destination. The moment the captain of the ship and a co-captain takes their eyes off the ship then the ultimate result will be chaos and lives may be destroyed. Both partners in the marriage are expected to play their individual and collective parts and to work ultimately together to make sure that they- along with their loved ones reach a destination that will bring happiness and prosperity to their lives even to the end of time.

FORSAKING ALL OTHERS

If you notice your partner no longer shows affection and support in the relationship, then it's time to make sure you pay attention to the red flags. If your partner brings back old, bad behaviors or takes on new negative behaviors that affect your marriage and maybe your loved ones then it's time you begin to seek professional help at any cost possible. If you notice your partner is hiding their cell phone from you, and not being transparent about the content that is on their phone, then it's time you begin to question things and to make sure that your partner and yourself have a dialogue about the reason for that lack of transparency and to make sure that you are not hiding things from each other that will affect the marriage adversely.

Communication and honesty are critical in any marriage, otherwise there will be room for doubt lack of trust and lack of confidence that will ultimately ruin the marriage. If you notice that your partner no longer shows interest or willingness to spend quality time with you, or they are spending more time hanging out with friends, colleagues, or family members than with you, then it's time you begin to observe the red flags and noticed that there are now room for other things and individuals to invade the health and growth of the marriage.

If you noticed that your partner is not as attractive like the day you met them, then it is time the two of you begin to seek professional counseling and take time to reevaluate your own thoughts and sit with your partner and share how you feel about him or her. Hopefully, your partner will listen to you and both of you can work together to overcome such feelings. As human beings we age and grow; however, we tend to neglect the fact that we change emotionally, physically, mentally, and spiritually as life goes on.

It is the job of each partner to recognize and appreciate the weaknesses and the strengths of each other and help each other to become better and to do better so that both can grow together to overcome all the odds that will ultimately work against the marriage. The goal of any marriage should be to enjoy the experiences with each other and make it all the way to the end with love, joy and happiness, regardless of what life may throw at the marriage.

FORSAKING ALL OTHERS

Sometimes, it gets a bit difficult to release yourself from your ex-partner. After being with the ex-partner for a while the emotions and feelings still linger and that may jeopardize the new relationship and marriage. If those feelings are entertained, then say goodbye to the current relationship and marriage. You can't serve two masters or share your heart with multiple people. It will destroy what you are investing into, and soon you may lose one or both persons. You stand the risk of being alone and possibly seeking another relationship to fill the void. When your spouse becomes extremely comfortable with the ex-partner, then it's quite possible a continued interest and relationship may blossom into what you never want to see or hear. When your spouse no longer wants to do anything with you or sometimes does things without you or spends more time with the ex-partner, then you should not blind your eyes to the inevitable.

When your spouse begins to be missing in action or not dedicating time to the things you both used to do, then you may want to ask questions or do more observation. If no building and planning are going on like you used to do together, then you may want to check into the matter and begin to get the attention of your spouse and begin to make it your business to find out why things have changed. These are certainly **RED FLAGS** and you must pay attention and follow-up with these behaviors, either by asking questions, monitoring, investigating or whatever you may see fit to get a better understanding of what is going on.

If you fail to see what's going on or fail to ask questions and just go with the flow, maybe one day it may be too late to do anything to improve the marital problems. Ignoring is a decision as well as making the efforts to observe and be proactive to get to the bottom of things to make sure that those reflags don't continue. If you love your spouse and you believe in the longevity of your marriage, then it's your business to preserve, provide and protect the marriage at all cost for the sake of marital bliss and fortitude. No one else can do a better job than you and your spouse to preserve and grow the marriage. Sharing your body with another person outside of the marriage is only assuring that the marriage is guaranteed to end at some point in time and by then there is nothing you or your spouse can do about it. If you do right by your partner and your partner does the same, then one can only expect the best of the marriage and the benefits that come with it thereafter. Once you put your heart, soul, mind, body and financial resources into your marriage, don't gamble it away and don't take risks with your future.

PUTTING THE KIDS ASIDE

We love our kids and God knows that they mean the world to us, but, there are times you have to put them aside and spend more time with your spouse. Why? Well, the kids will grow older and move on and by that time you are older and really don't want to start a new marriage or relationship with someone else after investing maybe 18 years or more with your children. You would want to make sure that your spouse is there with you to raise those little rascals. Who wants to raise kids by themselves especially if they have help and support from their spouse? We live in a society where family and spiritual value almost takes no prominence in our lives as they should. There are so many negative things that are destroying the very fabric of morale and values in our society, I am praying for this new generation along with our future as we get older. After all it will be frightening and challenging to live and survive the evil that will present itself to us in the future.

Love your kids. Train them well, and do your best to protect, preserve and provide for them. Dedicate more time to them. Be patient with them. Support each other. Establish and improve your partnership with each other. After all, when the kids leave, they will live their own life and you may need your spouse to be there for you all the way to the end of life. If you find that you love the kids much more than your spouse, and you treat your children better than your spouse, then such red flags must be recognized and be discussed before it's too late to fix the problem and restore the love, partnership and support of your spouse. Remember, you met, loved and married your spouse before you had children.

There was always the two of you before the kids' existence. Work on growing with your spouse and fix what needs to be fixed and never let anyone in this life turn your mind and heart away from your spouse, no matter what may occur in life. If you were married before and entered in to a new relationship with kids from your previous marriage or relationship, then you must recognize that both of you are taking on the family of your ex's from your previous relationship or marriage. You must now treat such a relationship and marriage as if you have just begun a new marriage with a brand-new family and never tell yourself that your new partner should have no part in the well-being and future of your children.

Respect must be shown at all times and working together is imperative in order to enjoy and appreciate your new partner and spouse. Both of you must serve each other and be there for each other's' kids; otherwise, you should never be in a new relationship or even get married if you are that selfish and care just for your kids only. If you find yourself despising your spouse's kids from a previous relationship or marriage, then it's time that such a red flag be recognized, and something must be done as soon as possible to fix the problem. Whatever the reasons are for you to manifest such feelings, then you must be honest with yourself and your spouse and talk about this matter in order to enjoy your marriage and your love for your spouse.

Whether the issue is with you, your spouse's children, or your spouse, honesty and truth is the best policy. Regardless of hiding the truth, you owe it to yourself, the kids and your spouse to talk about it and come to some consensus to make matters better for everyone at the end of the day. When you do right by others, then things will work in your favor at some point in time especially when you need it.

REKINDLE THE MARRIAGE

Sometimes you may not find your spouse as beautiful and attractive like when you first set eyes on them. Your interests may have been influenced by something or someone else. Your spouse has turned your mind away from loving them the way you used to love him or her. You may have grown tired of being with that person. You may have evolved and feel like moving on to something or someone else better than being with your spouse. You may tell yourself that you can juggle your marriage and something or someone else at the same time, just to satisfy your huge appetite.

Whatever it is, such red flags will have to be addressed by making the necessary effort to rekindle the marriage and the love for each other. If your spouse is not making the effort to rekindle the marriage and they have shown that he or she is very laid back and comfortable in the marriage and they don't need to spice up the marriage, then it's time you have a meeting and maybe get experts involved to help create an atmosphere that will contribute to the success of rekindling the marriage and restoring confidence, love and passion to the marriage.

We can take a chapter from the experiences of others we may know; whose marriage came to an end after failing to go above and beyond to rekindle the love and affection within the marriage. It's like trying to accomplish anything in life. You must have a plan, then do what is required. Never doubt or give up on what's left of the marriage. We understand that people will change for the better or worse while being married; however, marriage should not be treated like a car that ages over time and then later on you get rid of it because it does feel and ride the same way like when you first acquired it. Marriage is a recycling process. You take the old product and you bring it through a process, and no matter what you desire or plan to do with the old product, it will still bring great value to the new experience. Only when it goes through a process with purpose, goals, and anticipation for marital bliss and greatness. We all can evolve into someone better and greater than our current state.

All it takes is to realize that we need to make a change to become better than we are and be optimistic about what we can be and just become that very person. With God's help, I am certain that we can surprise ourselves and our spouse. One more thing: both spouses must go through the same process simultaneously in order to love, appreciate and support each other. There may be jealousy, hate or envy while your partner is going through this evolution, and you remain stagnant and complacent. That's why it is important that both persons have a dialogue and sometimes seek professional help and guidance to get through the process and transitioning together. You can begin with rekindling the marriage by surprising each other by the things you say or do that will make your spouse feel loved, appreciated and desired to go through the change with you.

PROTECTING THE MARRIAGE

Marriage is like a commercial airline, if both pilots fall asleep while flying, then certainly the plane will disintegrate into the earth and everyone will experience the pangs of pain and possible demise. Your marriage must be protected by you and your spouse all the days of your life. No matter how long your marriage maybe on cruise control, at some point, you will hit some turbulence especially while flying into a terrible and unexpected storm in your marriage. Furthermore, if you both of you don't protect the marriage, who will? Especially when the forces of evil come in through the front door and you didn't even recognize it, because you were too busy or blind to see what's happening. If your spouse gives more time and attention to his or her friends and frequently hangs out with them and tells you that they were friends before they met you, then such a red flag needs to be recognized and you must decide and act on it for your sake and the sake of the marriage. When the both of you got married, you left your extended family to begin a new family, not to mention leaving your best friends to make your new spouse your best friend.

If you choose to not make your spouse your best friend, then you got married not knowing the basic principles and morals of marriage. Now, you may not have been taught the basic principles and tenets of marriage. Well, it's not too late to learn and begin to do what's right to protect your marriage! Remember, you are not married to your best friends or your extended family. You have started a new beginning with someone you told that you love, cherish and adore until death do you part.

Never sell out your partner by telling your friends what's going on in your marriage and ask for their opinion. I am certain that they would share their opinion; however, bear in mind that their opinion should not have any bearing on your marriage at all. Never tell your parents and other family members to share their opinions either. Sometimes it's better to restrain your lips from sharing with others and seek professional, unbiased help in order to protect the marriage. Coming together to discuss and work together on protecting each other is the first step towards a strong marriage. Your spouse may be encouraged and look forward to working with you to protect and preserve your marriage. Both of you owe it to yourselves and no one else. If you love your spouse and want to be with him or her for the rest of your life, then the time is now to make the necessary move to love, cherish and protect the marriage no matter what may work against your marriage.

CHAPTER FOUR

RED FLAGS – Multiple Sexual Partners

You may be in a relationship and not know that your partner is bisexual. Such a secret must be discussed, and a decision must be made. Withholding the truth is just as dangerous as lying and deceiving your partner. One thing is for sure: the truth will come to light and, in many cases, the truth hurts and could cost someone their life. Secrets, secrets, secrets! They sometimes are our greatest enemy and the demise of relationships. The hidden, secret sexual urges or sexual sins must be shared between the partners for the sake of transparency, loyalty, trust and any possible hope for a future of togetherness. Not many people tell the truth about their sexuality or their sexual past.

You may or may not know someone who is married to the opposite sex, and yet share their life with someone else of the same sex. In many cases, there are signs of sexual appetite and preferences. This is more than one being homosexual or bisexual. This type of practice reflects confusion of preferences and maybe a total disregard for monogamy. Whichever way you may look at it, such practices are dangerous, and it puts lives at risk. A person in this situation obligated to share with their partner the hidden secret and behavior. The partner has the right to know and to decide. After all, this is a life changing activity, and the partner must be made aware immediately. Deceptions and lies only make the matter worse and cause a break-up to be eminent. Honesty is the best policy, regardless of the outcome after sharing or telling the truth. Withholding the truth or deceiving your partner can lead to hate, life-time resentment and pain.

Having sex with multiple people of the opposite sex at the same time maybe a curiosity or a continuation of ones' appetite. Whichever way you look at it, such urges and practices are quite common in our society, and many may have done so at some point in their life. Many may not feel morally convicted engaging with others in multiple sexual activities at the same time. Meanwhile, others despise the very thought and consider it evil and risky. No matter what, having multiple sexual partners can jeopardize a relationship and marriage. Those who have been down this road can share that if they could turn back the hands of time, they wouldn't have done what they have done. Some are experiencing deep emotional regrets and are paying the price. The trauma from their sexual choices or the decisions made by their partner has changed their life forever. In this case they are not happy and their guilt is overwhelming.

ENJOYING SWINGERS' CLUBS

There are many who enjoy going to a swingers' club with their partner at night or during the day, to share their partner with another and enjoy another partner themselves. Couples who practice such behavior see this as an opportunity for them to add fire to their relationship. Many would say this is therapeutic for their relationship and frequently visit these nightclubs to whet the appetite and clear the mind. If you ask your partner if they like swingers' clubs, and they express an interest in such activities then it should be considered a red flag, and such behavior must be looked into. Those who say that going to a swinger's club is therapeutic for their relationship must consider the possibility that they may have an attraction to others other than their spouse. Sex is quite therapeutic and it's good for the human anatomy, however someone who is open to the idea of sharing their partner with other people must recognize that they are jeopardizing their relationship or marriage. You may ask your partner if they have engaged in these activities in the past, and how they felt sharing their partner with someone else at such an event. If your partner is enthusiastic about such experiences again, then you may conclude that such behavior is a continuation, and this may be a problem in the future. This is a red flag that one must recognize, address and decide thereafter.

Your partner should value you and respect the relationship or marriage. If the relationship or marriage becomes toxic and overwhelming, then seek the counsel of a professional therapist or spiritual leader or even take some time away from each other to meditate and de-stress. Sometimes when you are in the moment of anger and pain you can't see things clearly or make the right decision. Taking a break from each other does not mean meeting someone when vulnerable and then sleeping with them in order to forget about the pain and hurt. Clearing your mind is critical; however, both partners must be on the same path of healing and eventual breakthrough. Honor your body and your marriage or relationship and don't be a contributor to the hurt and pain, both partners are going through. Too many relationships and marriages end with divorce, and many have regret thereafter. Making a hasty decision to break-up or divorce eventually costs both partners instead of benefiting them. Now, if your partner really wants a divorce, and you recommend counseling and so on, and your partner chooses not to participate, then there is no use fighting for something that has already ended. It takes two to make it work along with unconditional love, patience and understanding.

REACTION AROUND SIMILAR SEX – GAY AND LESBIAN

Sometime you'll never know if your partner is attracted to someone of similar sex. There are those who feel like it's okay so be sleeping with someone of similar sex and don't see that to be a problem. Many of us may have someone as a friend or colleague who is gay who feel so ashamed to come forward and tell their friends, colleagues, or partner who they really are. Sometimes gay people feel that if they are attracted to the opposite sex such behavior will cover-up their true sexual identity. We may know of individuals who are bisexual, but their partner does not know. Such behavior can be catastrophic to the immediate relationship and the lives of others. Our conversation is not about whether homosexuality is wrong or right, but rather is it the right thing to do by telling your partner that you are attracted to the similar sex which makes them a homosexual.

Sometimes you can just leave your partner to be in the company of someone of similar sex and observe the interaction and communication between both persons. A lot of touching of each other intimately, how they hug, and how they look into each other's eyes may be red flags that are telling you that the true identity of your partner is coming out at that moment in time. Further observation may be necessary as well as monitoring your partner's behavior in order to derive to a true assessment and finality that your partner is gay. Sometimes you can look up the types of clubs that they enjoy going to, and if he or she does not like to go to the same places you like to go, then you may want to find out why and perform more observation if necessary. Things like these cannot be overlooked and should be considered to be critically important. After all your future depends on it! You have to decide whether or not it's worth finding out your partners sexual preference and appetite.

Men and women who are attracted to similar sex may have had a dramatic experience in the past where sexual encounters are concerned. There are those who prefer or like to be sexually involved with someone of similar sex. There are those who are curious to find out what it is like to have sex with someone of the similar sex. Whatever it is, a person who is attracted to someone of similar sex struggles at first to identify themselves as a homosexual. Such dilemma may cause such person to deny such feeling and overwhelming urge. No matter how long the person tries to hide such urge and feeling, the truth will manifest itself at some point in time. There are those who are masters of disguise and pretense, however deep down in their heart and soul, they know that they must do right by the person there have been sexual intimacy with. Putting others' lives at risk is not cool and can never be right. If you or your partner is intimate with another person of the similar sex, it is important to let your partner know what's going, it's just the right thing to do.

SEXUAL ACTIVITIES AND PERFORMANCE

Sometimes you can tell whether or not your partner enjoys having sex with a person of similar sex or with someone else of the opposite sex or with multiple sex partners at the same time, based on their desired sexual activities and objects they like using during sexual intimacy. As human beings we tend to not pay attention to things as they happen; instead, we get caught up in the activities at that point in time. Too much sexual experience and very little sexual experience may hinder how we relate to our partner. Being open to new experiences may be a barrier or mere problem which may or may not affect sexual relationship with our partner. Whichever way you take it, it is important that we pay attention to our partners sexual activities or preferences, and that will tell us what to do or not do then. Nurturing the intimacy is critical to the long-term growth and development of the relationship and partnership.

If you recognize that your partner's desire to have intimacy with you has diminished, and they no longer want your attention, it is quite possible that something is there, and you must try to find out by asking or observing. These are red flags and it's time to make the move to make things work or turn the other way. If you go out with your partner, and he or she does not attend to you, but instead is responsive and friendly with others there, then it's quite possible that they are seeking attention elsewhere or already exploring other options. There is reason why people do what they do, and it is our business to recognize what's going on and do our best to improve the situation or seek a way of escape. Human beings give off red flags all the time, yet we fail to see and recognize them. Sometimes all you have to do is take a step back and observe for hours and maybe days, and you will begin to see the red flags and know what to do then. Never make an immediate assumption first without having a dialogue with your partner. Communicating with your partner is critical to the decision making.

Now, if your observation and findings are accurate and you speak with your partner, and then realize they are not into you like before, then you can decide if you would recommend getting help or decide to adjust your life and move on. We have to give credit to the red flags we see and do whatever it takes to make a decision that will contribute value to your life and your relationship with your partner. Sometimes it may be a simple issue; however, it may overwhelm the mind and spirit of your partner or even yourself. Red flags do not always mean that there is something evil or wrong going on; it can also mean that you have a better understanding about what's happening and how it is affecting you positively or negatively. Everyone wants to be happy and wants the best out of life; nonetheless, no one wants to go through the challenges and disappointments of life. With the support and effort of your partner to do right by each other, all things are possible and the relationship will get better and be more successful.

CHAPTER FIVE

RED FLAGS – Lies and Deception

Sometimes, you may want to ask your partner a question twice on different dates, just to see if the response is the same or not. If the response is totally different from the first response, then it is quite evident that your partner lied to you and is hiding the truth. Hiding the truth is as dangerous as lying. Some people may not want to share the truth with you because they don't want to disturb your feelings or mind, so they withhold the truth. Now, if and when you find out the truth and found out that your partner knew what was going on and never told you, then is quite evident that you will never trust the person again. Once you find out that your partner has been keeping you in the dark, then it gives you room to suspect that they are people of disloyalty and dishonesty. These are red flags you must pay attention to when dealing with your partner.

DELIBERATELY LYING

Withholding the truth is a type of lie; however, if your partner continuously lies to you and never admit to it or does not have any remorse, then you have to decide on what's the next move regarding your future. Habitual liars will not only break your heart, but they will also cause you to never love or trust another human being. Whether your partner is trying not to hurt your feelings by lying to you or he or she is just a habitual liar, it does not matter, you deserve the truth and information to make a decision that will make a difference in your personal life. Some people believe that if you don't know then you won't feel the pain or experience something negative. No one deserves to go through such experience and such red flag must be addressed and a life changing decision must be made.

If your partner truly loves and appreciate you, then there must be a dialogue, understanding and effort to be done by each other no matter what. We live in a society where people believe that it's fine to lie to each other, and no one has to admit it to anyone. Well, no wonder why we have so many single moms, broken relationships, divorces and sexual transmitted disease. The children that are coming into this world are so hopeless and uncertain about their future success. When one parent of the family is no longer there, then this automatically affects the child (children) negatively. We owe it to each other and our children to do the right thing amongst ourselves.

PRETENDER AND DECEIVER

One of the most divisive practices that affect relationships are pretense and deceptions. One thing for sure, the truth will come out one day, and someone may not be happy with what they see or hear. Pretense is another form of lying and should not be taken lightly. If you recognize that your partner is a pretender, just once for the first time, then that is a red flag and you must ask yourself, whether or not you will be willing to live with that person for the rest of your life. Certainly, you have the right to bring things to your partner's attention, and based on what you have seen and heard, you must make a decision that will either mend the relationship or end it.

Your partner is either temporary or permanent, so you have to decide on whether or not it's even worth addressing or having the person in your life weeks down the road. Remember, your life and future will be affected by your partner's pretense. The only way you will have an idea about the outcome of your relationship, you must begin observation, investigation, monitoring, communicating and deliberating.

Now, if you are the pretender, and your partner does not know, then you are harboring the behavior that will one day destroy your relationship and hurt your partner for life. If you love your partner, then you do right by them and let them know what's going on. If you worked so hard to find someone who makes your life beautiful despite the various challenges you both experiences, then it is safe to say that you do your best to do right by your partner. We have the power to influence our future outcome and to enjoy the benefits thereof. Red flags give away the behavior of an individual. One thing for sure, red flags will compel others to raise questions and seek answers from their partner or friends. By saving ourselves the hurt, pain and disappointment, it is important that we do the right thing and be true to ourselves and others. Based on the quality of the relationship, some people will take advantage of their partner and affect their lives positively or negatively.

ACTION CONTRADICT WORDS

We might hear the phrase, "action speaks louder than words." Take it from me, that's a fact. Sometimes people tell us one thing, and later on we find out the truth. If your partner says that he or she loves you, and then you find out that they are cheating on you, lying to you, always pretending, deceiving you, taking advantage of you, using you for their own benefits, manipulating you, abusing you verbally or physically and so on, then those are for sure red flags. You must be ready to make a life changing decision that will either benefit you or the relationship. One thing is for sure: there are those who will be with us, walk with us, but are not for us. They will walk a straight path for a long time; however, the truth will come out, and you must decide on whether or not it's worth the time or effort to continue your life with such a person.

Giving a person all the time in the world to prove or show that they mean what they say can be a great tool to explore and wait to see the results thereafter. Many people don't realize that action is so effective and much more powerful than what they actually say. We are either the benefactors or the victim of our partners contradictory behavior and deceptive words. We have the right to address the matter and receive the truth from our partner.

How would we react if we found out that our partner told us one thing and then later on we found out that what they are saying contradicts what they did or are doing? How would we feel if we ourselves are the culprit who contradicts what we say by our actions, and our partner finds out? Would it be fair to anyone to spend the rest of their lives with such a partner? People want the best of life; however, they spend so much of their life and time doing and saying things that are contradictory to the truth. How many times do we as adults find ourselves in such situations and are the cause of a problem and later on feel bad about what we did, and wish we could turn back the hand of time to do the right thing? Perhaps we were victims to a situation where our partners action and words were not aligned and later on we were devastated and never trusted our partner again? How much contradictions one can take from their partner will determine the person's confidence and trust in the person who is the cause or the person who inflicts the pain. Red flags are messages that tells us that no matter what we are doing at that point in time, we must stop, reflect, communicate and make a life changing decision thereafter. After all, we owe it to ourselves and our future.

CHAPTER SIX

RED FLAGS – Investment Went Down the Drain

Sometimes you think to yourself that the person you meet will be the person you want to spend the rest of your life with. They may have all the things you are looking for in such a person and, then later on you find out that after so many months and years everything came suddenly to an end. What did we miss or overlook? Or was it just a blip in time and we had to have a reality check before we move forward or not with such a person? Obsession and infatuation have certainly gotten the best of most of us, and we just won't let go even when the red flags are right there in our face to the point that we can reach out and touch it. Our time, money and energy invested into a relationship must bring a return on our investment. In other words, we must reap nothing less than happiness, blessings and success when connecting our lives with someone we have chosen to share the rest of our life with. We must value our time, appreciate our hard-earned income, and enjoy the sharing of our mind, body and soul with the person we share our being with.

MEN'S INVESTMENT

Men, you must understand that the day you meet a lady, it will cost you beginning on the first date, while you are dating her for weeks and month, when she becomes your significant other, during engagement, up to the time of the wedding, while you are married to her and even more after going through a divorce and after the divorce and raising kids with her. Men, you must ask yourself if you are ready for such a financial journey and commitment. These items I mentioned will occur, and you must understand it will cost you at some point of the journey. I'm not scaring you, however I am informing you with the inevitable. Dating, relationships, and marriage can be beautiful; however, it comes with a cost and it does require you to put your heart, soul, mind, and financial resources into it for the rest of your life being in it.

Now, it is important that before you begin such a journey, you must pay attention to the red flags as you go through any journey with such a person of interest. Note, the deeper you go, the more you are committing and investing into the journey with her. It does not make sense fooling yourself to think that things will get better over time when no one wants to spend the time to change and improve themselves and character. Men, if your partner has a list of items on a checklist that you must meet and when you pull out your check list, you found out you can't even get past the first three items on your list as it pertains to her, then you must run for your life! Don't fool yourself into thinking that she will change over time and satisfy at least fifty items on your list.

Men, if you don't see similar good qualities in your mother in your partner, then that's a red flag, and you must not take things for granted and compromise. You may find yourself regretting that you made such a move to continue with her. She may be so beautiful and satisfies your sexual desires and passion; however, after all that's over, can she do the things that will make your life better or enhanced? Is she a partner who you can trust and will take charge when you are not around? Does she make the relationship, marriage and family beautiful and makes you feel like maintaining a lifelong relationship and marriage with her? She must possess those qualities that complements your growth and development over time. She must be in for both of your interests and not just hers alone. Is she driven by material things like money and vanity? Is she faithful? Is she a ride or die partner, or will she bail out on you when times become difficult for both of you? These are things you must pay attention to and look for the red flags as they occur and decide if you want to go the expensive way or the way that will bring a bright future despite the cost involved.

WOMEN'S INVESTMENT

Giving our bodies, mind and heart to another human being must mean something valuable to us. There are too many pains, hurt and evil in our society that will destroy us and all that we have worked for in life. Why throw that all away because of how we are feeling and the lack of knowledge? Why invest in a relationship or marriage that's going nowhere? Are we blinded or obsessed with someone who inflicts pain and chaos in our lives? Are we desperate or just don't know any better? Whatever it is that is impairing our abilities to make sound decisions, we must avoid and pay attention to the red flags that are always before us.

Ladies, let's face it. For those of you who can have a child, bear in mind that it is quite likely that you may walk away with children after the relationship or marriage ends. The next thing thereafter is that you have to raise them as a single mom or perhaps get involved with another male partner to help you raise your children. You may still have your ex-partner or husband work with you to raise your kids together; however, it is not the same and the children will be going through the price of separation or divorce. What if your new partner wants to have kids with you and you don't want anymore? What will be the outcome of that relationship during the relationship? Don't you think it would have been better to wait and take your time before diving into a relationship or marriage? Wouldn't it be wise to be patient, observe the red flags, and then make a life changing decision? Are you in a rush to be in a relationship or get married? Are you lonely and can't handle the pain of being alone? Are you in heat, so that you just can't help yourself, and you try to have sex with someone just to satisfy that need? Whatever you are going through, you have to look at the cost and risk involved with the process, after all, money and time is valuable and should not be wasted especially with or on someone you will not be within the future.

TIME, MONEY AND YOUR LIFE

Think about it: your money, time and life are the most valuable commodities in your relationship, and you cannot afford to waste or lose them. Once they are gone, you may experience a tremendous loss that you may never regain, you may take a lifetime to get back to where you were before dating that person or you may rebound faster with the right person later on in your life.

Certainly, you might have heard or know someone who have been through a devastating experience which cost them a great deal and they are still feeling the side-effects of the pain after so many months or years. You may even be a victim to the situations share in this narrative and you are struggling to get to that place of comfort after the pain that was inflicted on you. You may have honestly committed a lot into your relationship and marriage and things end up sour or destructive and here you are today: unhappy, bitter, alone, hopeless, uncertain. Perhaps you have even changed your life drastically to have the desire for someone else of the same sex.

If you are currently in a relationship or marriage it is time to pay attention to the red flags and do what is important to improve it or starting making a decision that will save you additional cost, embarrassment, or further pain. It's never too late to starting doing something about your relationship and marriage and pray that the best will occur in your life. Many divorces occur and end up with partners finding an escape route or exploring other options that present themselves. Nowadays, people don't work on their relationship or marriage, because they have options, don't see the need to continue, or just being selfish and for themselves. Whichever may occur, red flags are indicators that one must pay attention to, observe and communicate with your partner. After addressing the matter, the next step is for both partners to decide to do right by each other or discontinue the journey with each other. Remember: red flags are not always bad indicators; however, they are there to help us become aware of what's going on and try to address them and reap the benefits thereafter.

CHAPTER SEVEN

RED FLAGS – Children and Influences

We must submit that today our children are so influenced by what's going on in high school, middle school and elementary school. We have to recognize that our children are slowly becoming their environment, and if we don't take the time to find out what's going on with them soon very soon we may be losing our children to everything that is completely wrong. Later on, we shed tears because we have lost them over time. We must understand also that our children are exposed to other children's' lifestyles that they bring from home into classroom and into the school setting overall. What goes on in the home, kids then go to school and tend to verbalize it or demonstrate to their peers and if their peers are not strong enough they'll accept it, receive it, and make it become a part of what these children are sharing with your children.

What children are reading, hearing, and watching is very much influencing how they perceive things and take these things to heart. Not only that, children are not only learning from their peers in schools today, but also, they're taking information and knowledge from what their teachers believe and practice that is shared in the classroom that you and I are never privileged to see and hear when those classroom doors are closed. If you noticed the behavior and the thought processes of these children today you will see that they may not sound like the children we have been raising due to the fact that they're so influenced by what they are hearing, seeing, and experiencing on a daily basis.

We are slowly losing our children to the things that they are inundated with and the things that their exposed to on a daily basis in schools and the community when we are not around. We must decide as parents to choose between earning an income and losing our children to the influences that are in our society that are slowly taking our children away from us. When are so busy or spending a lot of time having fun and doing things that makes us happy and not taking the time to know what's going on in our children's lives surely one day we'll wake up to realize that our children are not alone, anymore.

SOCIAL MEDIA AND KIDS

Our children are spending a tremendous number of hours every single day on Snapchat, Instagram, Facebook, and Twitter instead of spending actual time learning and advancing their knowledge to become a successful businessperson in the future. The social media activities that they are engaging in every single day for several months are taking away their cognitive ability to interpret and to communicate effectively to individuals face-to-face and in settings that require them to enunciate and articulate in a way that reflects cognitive advancement. On social media, one will recognize that children's activities are not monitored by parents. There is no parental guidance or protection on what these children are seeing, reading, and hearing on social media. Our children are exposed to feeds of knowledge and information and data and pictures that are not conducive for their moral and ethical development. If you take a good look around you, our children are so inundated and focus on their cell phones as if they're addicted and find it very difficult to detach themselves to take a break and really engage. They often interact unaware of their physical surrounding and reality.

One may agree that social media is making our children become very lazy and unproductive. They may not do well in school and may also not be able to be effective communicators and benefactors of knowledge and demonstrators of that knowledge. Our children nowadays are not driven and passionate about careers, entrepreneurship, and success. Many of them don't even want to leave home. They want to stay home with parents and not be bothered with responsibilities. Our children have become so comfortable, laid-back, passive, unproductive, and lack any urgency to get up out of the nest and to go begin the future and start a new family. Our children are so caught up with social media and indulgences with their peers that they don't see anything else other than just enjoying the world they have created for themselves.

SEXUAL PREFERENCES

Our children are becoming more confused as to what their sexual orientation or identity is. More and more children today in high schools are finding themselves influenced by members of the similar sex to believe that it's okay to be with someone sexually of the same sex. Our children are finding it very difficult to not fit if they are to be a part of a sexual orientation group. They may not know that very soon they will become very influenced and begin believe that it's okay to be attracted to someone of the same sex. Our children do not have to be exposed to today's sexual orientation activities intimately or sexually in order for them to start thinking that they should love and be with someone of the same sex. We have to understand that. Peer pressure and bullying is quite common and popular in high schools today, and parents must be aware that these things are happening quite frequently in high schools today more than we can ever imagine. If we, as parents, fail to find out what's going on in the lives of our children pretty soon our children manifest bad behavior.

Not only are you going to be surprised, but you would find out that we have lost them because we have not been engaged in their lives for a very long time. We must ask ourselves some of the questions that are needing to be answered. Why are we not involved in our children's lives? Why are we afraid of asking our children questions that are important? Why are our children fearful of telling us what's going on in their lives? Why are our children confused as to whether or not they should love the opposite or the same sex? Why are our children interested in individuals of similar sex? What are we afraid of as parents? Does it or does not really matter to us? What are our children experiencing at schools today? If we fail to be parents now, don't try to be parents later when you're ready lost them.

COLLEGE AND CAREERS

Not every child is easily influenced - especially if they come from a solid home. One of the things you must put into consideration is that our children should be nurtured and talked to. The need to be prepared for careers and possible business opportunities in the future. Our children should be focusing on graduating from high school and going on to some institution of higher learning that prepares them for professions and careers that's going to help them to be successful in the future. As parents we should introduce our children to college catalogs, conferences, webinars, networking events, and programs that are going to get their mind stimulated and ready for college.

What we would notice is that our children are not so much focused on what particular college they should get into or what particular major they should focus on or what type of industry they should prepare themselves for in the future. Instead, children are so comfortable going through the motions in school. When they get home, they are spending so much time on social media, video games, or anything that's unproductive or not stimulating and not educational and that are not preparing them for the future. We must ensure that we're preparing the minds, the hearts, the bodies, and the souls of children to be healthy, moral, and ethical for the world of opportunities and success.

OBEDIENCE AND DEFIANCE

Our children are becoming more disobedient and more defiant more than we can ever imagine. When me to try to correct them or try to guide them, they tend to question us as to why are we are telling them as if we have to explain to them the opposition regarding the matter at hand. We may have seen in public on TV or even in the household that some children act as if they are the parents and parents are the children. It has come to a point where parents apparently have surrendered their position to their children and are afraid to scold their children with words or physicality in order for these children adhere to our instruction, guidance and principles. When our children decide to not hear us anymore and rebel against what we instructed them to do, we must understand that it has gotten to a point where not only are our children out-of-control but they have been highly influenced by individuals outside of the home.

Whenever our children begin to tell us or show us that they are right and we are wrong or to challenge our authority and instructions, we have to recognize that these are red flags that need to be addressed immediately before it gets any worse. If we fail to take the time to be around our children, ask them questions, engage in their lives, and teach and guide them, then most certainly as they get older it's going to be very difficult for us to be parents anymore. Ask yourself the question: are the parents or are we children? It is time that we start to take control of what goes on in all our lives and to monitor our children's activities. We're solely responsible for them and no one else.

DRUGS, VIOLENCE AND LOSS

In schools today, children are exposed to drugs and violence which are leading to their demise. The fact is that we don't know what's going on in schools today. We don't know what our children are exposed to, and we don't know who their friends are. It is quite difficult for us to know whether or not our children are exposed to drugs and violence. Every year hundreds and thousands of children across the country and across the world have died because of drugs and violence and we look to our system to fix the problem not realizing that we as parents have a moral obligation to make sure that our children are safe and are not exposed to these things.

All it takes is for children to be exposed just one time to any type of drugs at any given time. Who wants to lose a child to drugs? No one! We depend on the schools and we depend on government leadership, and still our children are exposed to drugs. They are slowly creeping on to school campuses and into the hands of children who later on are admitted to rehabilitation centers or die. We must pay attention to unusual behaviors and tendencies of our children and to question their behavior and, if need be, to take them to seek professional help. It's a painful experience to see your child's suffering and you can do very little or anything to take away their pain.

Instead of waiting for something to happen to our children, let's be a bit more proactive and engage in our children's lives and begin to be parents and allies by teaching them and guiding them on the right path in life. We must remember: children are children. They're not fully-grown people where we expect them to act grown up and understand things as a full-grown adult. We must recognize they are young and they are not adults even though they may dress and act like grown adults. They are not! They are children, and they need teaching and guidance throughout their youthful days. Parents should be parents and children should be children. If we see that children are displaying erratic behaviors and tendencies or have been very isolated and tend to lock themselves away in their room it is our business to make sure we know what's going on. We must go beyond those bedroom doors that separate us from them during the day and especially at nights. These red flags are indicators that we as parents must intervene and be there for our children.

FAMILY AND QUALITY TIME

It is important that we spend quality time with our children. We are family despite the fact that we have to earn an income and take care of the family every week. Sometimes, it may be difficult, and sometimes we may have to time to spend with our children but instead we spend most of our time away from them and are not there to guide, protect, and preserve them. Dedicate specific days for specific events for your children. Dedicate a single day for you and the children to go places and enjoy each other outside of the home. Sometimes taking a break from stressful activities will also help us heal as parents. We know this, but there are so many demands on our time and energy by others outside or from within the home; therefore, we have to make it our business to dedicate our time and energy to our family and especially to our children.

When we take the time to have eat with our children, and at the table have a dialogue with them, laugh with them, and have fun with them, it makes every single person feel good to be around each other. The children look forward to that more than you can ever imagine. As parents, it's beautiful to sit and look at our children who we have brought into this world and then show them how beautiful they are in eyes. It is our business and prerogative to ensure that we enjoy every moment in time with our children and to take pictures and videos of those moments. Those moments will never occur again. Spending quality time with our children may well save our own lives as parents. No quality time with children equals a family that's on the verge of demise.

TEACHING AND UPBRINGING

Teaching our children to know and understand what is right from wrong is very important for us to do as parents and guardians. Our children look to us for leadership and guidance and whatever they see, in many cases, they end up doing in future. Teaching our children how to make effective and correct decisions may well save their lives in the future. Our children will follow our lead when we demonstrate and practice things that are right - morally and ethical. If we show them the process that leads to success, it is quite evident that our children will follow our lead and, in many cases, will appreciate what we have done for them.

Our children will never forget their upbringing, the lessons they learn from us, or the principles that we share with them for the rest of their natural life. It's a beautiful thing to see the product after you work in your children. As parents, we want our children to be better than us and as parents we want to celebrate and enjoy their success in our older days. Let us teach children to think like leaders, to think like a Chuck Norris, to think like experts, and to think like professionals. We have already conditioned them to believe that they are what we influence them to become. That is considered greatness. Our children are an extension of us; therefore, we must take pride in training them and preparing them to be better than we could ever be in life.

CHAPTER EIGHT

RED FLAGS – Best Friend

When you have a best friend sometimes is hard to accept the fact that they will lie to you and deceive you. We are so forgiving and forgetful, we just keep going on with our friendship and make things interfere with our friendship. Almost all of us do that and at some point, and get hurt and suffer depression. After all we never expected our best friend to do the thing they did to destroy the friendship. The boy and girl code say that we are to be loyal to each other even if we are disloyal to others. You don't take your best friend's girl or you don't have sex with your girlfriend's man. These are no-no actions that should never happen. You never rob your best friend or hide the truth from your best friend and watch them walk into a trap. Loyalty and trust are everything in a best friend relationship, right?

LONG TIME FRIENDSHIP

When you started out your best friendship, both friends are inseparable, ride or die, and partner in crime, so to speak. In other words, you have your best friend's back, no matter what. Both you and your best friend know the innermost deep secrets about each other and as such will never be uttered into the hearing of another - especially from your lips. Some long-time best friendships end up thicker than flesh and blood relationship. No matter what anyone says, you value your friendship and, in many cases, you might take a bullet for your best friend. No one can speak badly about your best friend or try to hurt your best friend. No, that will not happen in your presence. You may do some damage for your best friend in the name of protecting and preserving your best friend and their good name.

We become so blind, that we will never imagine that our best friend would take our trust and do anything to impair or destroy our friendship. We are never ready or prepared for a total let down, deception or set-up by our best friend. I honestly believe that, many best friend relationships get destroyed because of greed and selfishness. What do you think? There has to be a great and compelling reason for a best friend to sell-out his or her friend and destroy the friendship. Not when you are best friends since childhood. You just don't get up one day and say that the friendship is over and move in the other direction without feelings and remorse. You believe that big things will happen for the both of you, and everyone will enjoy the life that is designed and waits ahead for both of you. You consider your best friend family, and the one who will make sure that you are at the place you want to be and enjoy the rest of your life. Your friendship means everything to both of you; therefore, chaos is not an option.

If you find that your friend is doing things secretly and not having a dialogue with you about anything, yet he or she wants every detail about what's going on in your life, then such person is a crooked character and should not be entertained. If you have a best friend and such a person shares your conversations with others and pretends to your face that nothing went down, then such a red flag is to be looked into and something must be done. If your best friend changes on you after earning lots of money and other resources and neglects to remember that you helped them to get to that point in life, then you may want to re-evaluate your friendship and make a decision that is life-changing. If your best friend bails out on you when your back is up against the wall, or when you are facing difficult moments, then such red flag should not be overlooked or ignored. Your friendship is either on the verge of dissolution or needs to be adjusted. Whatever is going on with your best friend that is negatively working against your friendship, it must stop and something must be done before the matter gets worse.

BEST FRIENDSHIP EXPIRATION DATE

It may be hard to believe, but there may be a time where your friendship must come to an end in order for a new one to be birthed. Just like couples can grow out of love, best friends frequently do the same. Is it because of what each other does to each other, or is it that people are inconsistent in their friendship or with anything in life? Is it that people are just failures or cannot be trusted? Whatever it may be that causes people to jeopardize their friendship, it's no surprise that it happens all the time. The question is, when bad things occur during the friendship, what does one do then and how do things get better? Red flags will present itself and if we overlook them they are quite possible by the time we find out what happened and how bad it is, it might be too late to fix it or do anything to reconcile with your best friend.

How important is our best friendship to us will be determined by how we treat each other and whether or not we are in each other's best interests? When your friend can't forgive you for a mistake you made and decides to just end the relationship, then you may want to consider the fact that the person was not really a good friend. There are many things that can be done to make things right, better and work. Both friends should do right by each other, no matter what. Forgiveness is one thing, but forgetting is another. How you want to be treated will determine how well the friendship works and gets better in the future.

WHY HAVE A BEST FRIEND IF YOU CAN'T TRUST PEOPLE?

Trust is so important in any relationship. Without trust it is like trying to drive a car without an engine; there is no hope of getting to our destination. Many of us have had bad experiences with best friends; however, the relationship ended because it was violated and dissolved. Human behavior has everything to do with how long friendship lasts. If you have a friend who leaks personal and private information about you to others, one may want to recognize, monitor and contain the situation before it becomes a serious problem. Such red flags should not go unnoticed and ignored. If your friend is constantly misleading you and take your friendship with them for granted then it's time you notice the red flag and make it your business to do something about the matter before it becomes chaos.

Why should we even trust people in the first place if we know for sure that they will fail us? We have seen and experienced the pain of betrayal and disappointment from people who we have trusted and have had confidence in. Is it worth living alone without having someone in our lives to talk to and share our personal challenges and experiences with despite the negative events that transpired in our lives? Whatever you do, it is important to realize that we are humans and everyone has weaknesses, and will fail at some point. At the same time not everyone wants to hurt us intentionally. Once we are in this human body of ours we have to recognize that we will even fail ourselves. Therefore, we can either forgive others for the wrong they did to us or not. What we must not do is judge everyone else in life because of the experiences we had with someone else in our past. Every one of us have crossed each other's path for a reason, whether we know it or not or believe it or not. We can lead others by example and do right by them and they by us.

CHAPTER NINE

RED FLAGS – Identification and Rectification

WHAT IS LIFE?

Life is a gift and should be protected with all that is within us. Don't waste it and certainly don't sell it to others who will eventually use us and make a profit off of us. The thing about life is that when it is ruined or utterly destroyed there is no hope or possibility thereafter to start over again. It's just over. Life is given to us to identify and benefit from in the long run. Life surely will present to us both negative and positive experiences. All we need to do is learn from the negatives and benefit from the positives. Problems and struggles will not last always and forever. They occur for a reason and we must learn how to handle them and seek help to overcome them.

We were born to survive and accomplish things in life. You must believe that and pursue your goals and happiness with as much help, guidance, and support as possible. Every successful person has a story to tell and above all they will agree that they never stop believing and pushing themselves to greatness. They may also tell you that they have failed many times, however they got help and they made it to where they are today. They will also tell you that they have taken on new challenges and problems, however because of their previous experiences, they are handling things much better and more professionally. Each of us must realize that we have it in us to overcome every challenge and obstacle. All we need to know is how to find a way to overcome them and seek help while we can.

No one person ever becomes great without other people. Everyone becomes great because of human intervention, involvement, engagement, guidance, support, mentorship, or coaching.

Whenever someone says that they are self-made, I wink at their limitation of thinking. No one is self-made. We are influenced and affected by someone else's contribution of value to our lives. We owe it to our self to aspire to greatness and thank those who helped us to get to that place where we wanted to go. Humility is vital, and we must practice it in life. Otherwise, we miss out on some great experiences and relationships in life.

WHO ARE YOU?

Who are you? You may or may not have asked yourself the question; however, it must be asked and when you find out who we are for sure, then you should begin or continue to aspire to be at a better place in your life. We were created and designed to be great at something, maximize it, and reap the benefits thereafter. You have so much in you to offer; start finding out what that is and begin working on it and reap the benefits in the future. Could it be that you may have to revisit your kindergarten to 12th grade years to find out what you were good at then and begin working on and developing it today? Let's face it: you don't have the time or luxury to waste another day not trying to figure out who you are, what is your innate qualities, and how to develop them and begin reaping the benefits from your labor. You must start today in order to have a jump start which leads to a place of greatness. It's attainable and must be explored.

Are you someone who enjoys solving problems, or someone who helps people to better themselves or someone who has the ability to create things that will improve how organizations do things or are you someone who makes people feel better about themselves? No matter what, you owe it to yourself to make a difference in your life first and then others. The time is now, and you might love what you learn about yourself. Begin today to learn more about yourself and the capabilities you possess and what to put into full gear and enjoy the journey of self-discovery. You may begin asking family members, friends and associates about what they think you are good at doing and what qualities they see you possess and how they affect them personally and professionally. You might be blown away by what you find out about yourself.

WHAT IS YOUR PURPOSE

Living without purpose is like having this beautiful ship, and it's just sitting there in the water without fuel. Purpose is fuel, and it takes you exactly where you need to be. Many of us are living without purpose and perspective and that's why we are still searching for answers to remove the void in our lives. Some of us are trying to find ourselves. Meanwhile some of us are struggling to believe in ourselves. Wherever we are today, it's time we live with purpose and perspective. After all, we are people with extraordinary abilities, skills and know-how. Are you a person of service to others or a person of life and hope to many? Well, you must find out and begin living instead of just existing. Some of us are just going through the routine of life and not living or living with purpose.

Sometimes all it takes is for us to give our comfort zone a rest and begin to explore going on an adventure to find out what your gift, calling and purpose is in life and enjoy the moment in time. We see millions of people who are making a difference in our lives and others today and will continue forever. Why not find out what it is that we can contribute and leave this world with a legacy? Imagine that you are the person who gave life and hope to someone who needed your contribution and later on share their thankfulness with you and will never forget about what you have done for them, and how you have changed their lives forever. The red flags in your life are there to help you identify and rectify the issues in your life. You have so much to offer; it's time you turn those red flags and limitations into benefits, solutions and profit. Begin today, and you may be encouraged by what you have discovered about yourself.

THERE IS SOMEONE FOR YOU

Don't let anyone tell you that you are a nobody, and that you are a waste of their time. Only weak people speak like that, and they want to trap someone into their limited way of thinking. You are special and that there is someone out there waiting to meet you and would love to be a part of your life. You are wonderful, and deserve the best in life. Now, if you are with someone and they tell you that they love you and you believe that with all your heart, yet they treat you badly and bring you more pain than you can ever imagine, then despite how much love you have for that person, you must come to terms with the fact that your pain may not just be mental and psychological for a long time, but in many cases it may lead to pain from physical abuse. Relationships of this kind frequently end up with someone dying and the other end up in prison.

You must respect and value who you are each an every day. Our society has become brainwashed into thinking that being vain, materialistic, and immoral is the way to go. If selling your body and soul is the way to go, not very long from now, you may commit suicide or remain in depression. Why do we believe that we should be and live like everyone else who does not believe and practice good family values and ethical principles? There is more to life than looking good physically, having a lot of money, and exposing your body and mind for pleasure. Lots of us are working towards self-destruction, and we fail to even recognize that. I've seen wealthy people live long, enjoy their wealth and have high moral and family values. Yes, these wealthy folks believe in being and living differently; however, they try to live a secluded and dignified life. They believe that they are special and superior. In other words, they believe in the power of their family name and preserving it by being exceptional and not being like everyone else.

You have to ask yourself every now and then, who are you and how valuable you are to yourself and others? Are you connecting your life with someone who is working against your progress and value? Are you working on evolving and becoming a better person? Are you investing into your life and future? Are you living in fear and anxiety? If you are a victim to these questions, then it's time to realize that these are red flags, and you need to make a change. Change is important and enjoying one's future is way more important in life. You can't afford for another human being to alter or take away the blessings that await you in life.

Work towards being free from the spell and influence of someone who is toxic and dangerous to your life. Don't think about making the change. Just do it and don't look back. Once you make that bold and critical move, then at first you may feel like you are alone, and you just can't make it. If you feel that way, why? Because you are almost there, and you are not sure what to expect. What you will experience after such a journey is the feeling of joy, happiness, hope, and the mindset to be successful. It will be a whole lot better once you let go of the evil that's hanging over your head.

CHAPTER TEN

BEING WISE IS BETTER THAN BEING SMART

Do you know someone who is smart but does stupid things? Do you know someone who is educated but made uneducated decisions that cost them in the long run? It's good to be educated and smart, but it's best being wise and make great decisions that will bring benefits and blessings to everyone including yourself. When you look at society today, most people think that they are smart by the things they do or even say, but yet the price they pay for making poor choices is overwhelming and incomprehensible.

In everything we do we must consider the fact that we have to think about the end result and the benefits thereof and how it will affect others. In order to make effective decisions, we must have enough information and knowledge that will further prepare us for the outcome were expecting. It's not enough just to have a desire and it's not enough just to want something, but it's important that we know and understand what must be done in order for us to reap the benefits of our labor. Wisdom tells us but everything we do should not only working our best interests but also in the interests of others. We all have access to knowledge and information that can enabled us to make good decisions. We must have a plan of what we must do and where we are heading to. It makes no sense that would just rely on our limited information and limited understanding yet make a life-changing decision. Red flags are indicators that tell us that we must stop, listen, observe, monitor, and make the right decision that's going to be relevant to our well-being.

It is time that we make the right choices. Choose wisdom to lead us into greatness. We have made so many bad decisions in the past that it's time we pay attention and watch what is going on around us and in our lives and begin to take control of our lives and our future. We owe it to ourselves and others to do the right thing and reap the benefits thereof. No one knows like we do the pain and suffering we had to go through in order to get to where we are today. Now is the time for us to be wise in our doings and to not let anyone take advantage of us and alter our future. No more will we give the power of our life to others to manipulate us and our future. Now is the time for us to live happily and enjoy life to its fullest no matter what we're going through in life.

INVEST INTO YOURSELF ALWAYS

It is time that we invest in ourselves by acquiring knowledge and surrounding ourselves with people that are in our best interest and want to see us grow and evolve into greatness. We have come to a point in our lives where we realize that red flags are our guide to make great life-changing decisions. Our enemy will become powerless if we take control of our life and do what we please with own life. Embrace and choose life and remember life will do what you tell it to do once you understand the dynamics of life and the giver of life. Once your mind is transformed and you begin to do what you must do then life will respond in your favor. You are the master of your fate, and the solution to your problems. You are the one who was the key to open any door that is accessible to you.

Once upon a time you were not paying any attention, but today you believe in red flags and you believe red flags will get you where you need to go. The red flags that you recognize will always remind you of the pain you suffer and the errors you made and what you must do did not repeat those vicious mistakes. No more would you become a slave to red flags, but rather you'll use red flags as a guide you need you to greatness.

After understanding what you must do in order to be great you must remember that to be great and successful you need people to help you get there. So you may close the door that was toxic to your well-being and access new doors that will create opportunities, happiness, joy and success. Your future is bright, and you have what it takes to experience the outcome you want to experience. Now go pursue your dreams and aspirations and if there are things that you must fix then fix them. If those contributors to the problem do not want to make the change, and they desire to maintain evil in their lives then it's time for you to make the right decision which is going to work in your best interests and the interests of others.

ABOUT THE AUTHOR

DR. LESTER REID
Transforming Lives and Organizations

Dr. Lester Reid is a transformational leader and speaker who believes in the power of knowledge, education, innovation, transformation and Almighty God. He believes that once a person immerses themselves into the power items mentioned above, it is inevitable that one can master their faith, dreams, purpose and destination. Dr. Reid has transformed the minds of hundreds of individuals nationwide and internationally at: conferences, seminars, workshops, symposiums, colleges, university, religious and corporate organizations. His transformational speaking and training have earned him revisits and honors.

Dr. Reid is an author of several published work, he is a life coach, financial and business expert, entrepreneur, professional accounting, college professor, transformational and motivational speaker. His academic and professional background has earned him the respect, appreciation and acknowledgement in the fields of: psychology, organizational behavior, scholarship, financial management, business management, religion, counselling, adult and higher education. He has taught, supervised, mentored, coached, trained and developed doctoral, masters, Executive MBA and undergraduate students at public, private, Christian, and HBCU's colleges and universities nationwide and internationally. He has developed and taught innovative and cutting-edge courses for colleges and universities, nationwide and internationally in psychology, organizational behavior, accounting, finance, business management, federal taxation, economics, entrepreneurship, technology, organizational behavior, adult and higher education.

Dr. Reid enjoys teaching, mentoring, coaching, speaking, training and developing, and preparing individual for greatness and success. He is called to serve and help individuals and organizations to improve and become successful. His work has spoken for itself by those who have experienced his teachings, training, mentorship and coaching on: www.ratemyprofessors.com at various colleges and universities. Those who experienced Dr. Reid's work will share that his transformational teaching and speaking approach has changed their lives forever.

Dr. Reid is open to invitations to speak and train individuals at special events, nationwide and internationally. He will be delighted to make a difference in your audience life at that moment in time which will advance the human mind to greatness.

Follow Dr. Reid on Twitter and on WWW.GHEIevent.com.

Made in the USA
Monee, IL
03 February 2022

90580926R00092